Psychic Reality,

An introductory course

By Peter F Kelly

Other titles available by Mr. Kelly

1. Warning, My Philosophy
2. Infinite Light, Poems to the Self
3. Secrets of the Grapevine, the mathematical possibility of God
4. Hidden In Plain Sight, esoteric wisdom poems
5. Virtual World, a handbook for infinity
6. Esoteric Love Poems, an education in love
7. Infinity, reality beyond experience

Latent in all

The mind resides

Capable of headset

Mental bandwidth acts

Asleep in dreamers

Experiencing life

As sleepwalkers

In a waking dream

In use by psychics

Attained faculty

Realized potentials

Using mind's eye

All seeing

The subliminal

Mind's eye connection

Waiting for an approach

2

A shared organ

A shared view

A shared family

With all existing

Psychic mastery

Bestows on pupils

Whether all seeing

Or of smaller view

One with life

Pupil becomes

As mind grown

Into itself fully

Omnipresent

Omniscient

Omnipotent

Masters are

3

Pupils courting

Seeking love

Of themselves

The master mind

The lover's posture

Taking in approach

To relationship

Of pupil and mind

Pupil draws close

Recognizes itself

Comes to mind

Heart in hand

Mind sees

Knows itself too

Those that court it

Seek its love

4

Invisible

Elusive

Unknown

Power

Ceiling

Capacity

Maximum

Power

Quantum

Space

Infinite

Power

Magical

Fantasy

Esoteric

Power

5

One ancestor

One law

One knowledge

In common

One family

One gift

One mind

In common

One kind

One life

One abstinence

In common

One source

One matter

One power

In common

6

Role playing

Gaming

Posture performing

Lovers interact

What scenes

What teams

10

What scale

Lovers interact

Universal pictures

Populations

Omnipresent

Lovers interact

With props and sets

With gear and fields

With perfect mastery

Lovers interact

7

The line

The wheel

The population

Infinite

Numbers capacity

Multiplied by calculators

Time expanded

Infinite

Space

Area

Volume

Infinite

Power

Ability

Capacity

Infinite

8

Mind power

Force of will

Strength's seat

Knowledge amplified

Quantum force

Infinite volume

Space mass

Knowledge revealed

Live wire

Power on

Transformed

Knowledge secret

Special effects

Misdirection

Denials

Knowledge acts

9

Solitary applicant

Sole pupil

Individual aspirant

Hermit student

Loner

Recluse

Madman

Hermit potential

Mind

Higher power

God

Hermit's teacher

Lover

One

Master

Graduate

10

Controlled experience

Deliberate performance

Sting set act portrayal

Mental construct

Role play

Game action

16

Improvised

Mental acts

Mind powered

Mind machines

Mind technology

Mental life

Mind

Motor

Muscle

Mental anatomy

Safe to stage

Says the sage

Are allowed

Except in clubs

Laws clubs

Censor acts

Fine, penalize

Performances

In Godhead

Liberty abounds

Freedom found

Variety accepted

Drama, tragedy

Comical, romantic

All acts allowed

On God's stages

12

Incense, oils, candles

Herbs and spices

The four elements

Their magic taught

Behind the scheme

The fabled lore

Magical language

The true power

Auto suggestion

Self communication

Higher power requests

True magic's form

Belief essential

In your subliminal link

Your connection

To all seeing, all powerful mind

13

Death as a veil

Drawn between lives

A pregnant moment

A dramatic pause

Death an exit

From life's stages

To afterlife reception

And starting over

Death only temporary

Parting of companions

Until reunited again

On afterlife's shores

Death tragic

In its loss

From action

A player

14

Experience is illusory

To what degree

The ultimate question

Needing to be asked

Can you move a mountain

With just your mind

Can you fly into

Your mind's eye plane

How far is up

How low is down

Important questions

On the matter

If external reality

Infinite plane

Then a vast mind

Is the same

15

Impossible

Madness

Mistake

They say

There's no such thing

It can't be done

Foolish to believe

They add

Waste of time

A fool's errand

A mental disorder

They conclude

Fool's gold

Knowledge of infinity

Can be treated

In illusionists hands

16

Experience unyielding

Any confirmation

Infinite knowledge

Applicable

Can't move an ashtray

Can't get off the ground

Can't do a thing

Infinite knowledge teaches

Except the superimposed

On that in progress

Like a new explanation

For everything

With a warning

Experience a slave

Of its masters

To conform to their will

17

Steady your mind

In the candles flame

It's all in your head

To schools of thought

How strange a thought

It's in your mind

Everything occurs

In your life experiences

Stranger yet

What is possible

In your mind

In your illusion

Taught and skilled

What could you do

In your mind instead

Of just review as shown

18

The moon phases

Come and go

What of a mind

Is its life so

Unschooled, initiate

Novice, adept

Four stages

In mystery schooling

New, waxing, full

Then waning in its orbit

Both moon and students do

In their courses

How much light

Of life's mysteries

Do you possess

In your life

What type

Information

The star

In your life

Word of mouth

Education

Media distributed

Any other

Truth's followers

Its little sheep

Personally recognize

Truth and information

They are not the same

Truth is the facts

Information is words

That present data pictures

20

Who leads you

Instead of truth

Given as guide

Through all

What references

Given you

31

Instead of truth

Tables and volumes

What degree master

Of life's mysteries

Head of your school

Informing you

Are they spell bound

Studying an illusion

For its knowledge

Instead of infinity

21

Worlds in a dream

How valid the entities

How accurate the lessons

Learned there from

How much like a dream

Waking life beyond appearances

Occurring in your mind

Like another mind plane

Accepting the possibility

It may be a mental construct

How serious a study

Of mind relativity to be made

Guaranteed universals

Applicable everywhere knowledge

Knowledge true anywhere

That is knowledge of infinity

22

How difficult it may seem

To approach the mind

Behind reality beyond the scenes

So much a god in natures

Yet a relationship

Can be formed

Of oldest ancestor

Or even lover

Mind is source

Of your knowledge

And every act

It is no stranger

Come as a friend

Come as a descendant

Come as lover

But do come

23

Falling in love

With a companion

Always with you

Is easy to do

Courting

Romance

Easy acts too

For companions

Seeing beyond

Life's daily illusions

As theatrical acts

Clears the head

The invisible companion

Seen thus clearly

A playful monster

Easily loved

24

Making the commitment

To view life

As infinite reality

Alters your mind

Alchemical wedding

Turning all to gold

Superconductive

Of mind natures

Commitment's result

Making the habit

Of infinite review

Of that occurring

Yields a steady mind

In any situation

Free of confusion

Even if reality alters

25

Ceiling capacities

Maximum power

Infinite force

Describe mind's power

Master of illusion

Creator of experience

Reality programmer

Describe the mind

Master

Infinite Lord

God creator

Mind's been called

Ancestor

Companion

Lover

Mind can be

26

A secret love

Fills all life

Behind the scenes

To masters

Awaiting discovery

Kindling to a flame

Love's embers glow

Warming hearts

Ancestral deity

Loving generations

The secret knowledge

Of faithful hearts

Love everlasting

Held in store

For everyone

Unconditionally

Lovers possess

A spark divine

Touch of heaven

Within their breasts

Lovers can rise

Upon their love

Experience bliss

In love with life

Loves flames can melt

Your body and soul

Unite you with God

In its passion

Glowing embers

Of loves fire

Carry you through

Life's ups and downs

28

Fall in love

Stay in love

Expand your love

To include life

Climb on board

Loves sacred chariot

See all family

Love them as such

All family jewels

Life's population

Priceless assets

Each in its way

Each gathered

Each you keep

Increases your wealth

In family life

Loves power

Maintains creation

Supports all life

Keeps time flowing

Loves foresight

Comes prepared

Probes possibilities

Makes arrangements

Loves majesty

One ancestor

One kind

One family

Loves library

One wisdom

One knowledge

One law

30

The divine couple

Siamese twins

Sharing one mind

In two bodies

Like characters

In sleeps dreams

Sharing the mind

Behind appearances

Partners in life

Sharing time together

A plural noun

Omnipresence

From secret love

To passions embrace

Joined like logs

In one bon fire

Loves tiniest spark

Can light the torch

That guides the lover

To heavenly bliss

Life realized

Loves expressions

Its games and role play

Banks the fire

Glowing embers form

In long burning fires

Fed fuel routinely

Like an eternal flame

Love meant to grow

From beloved to family

To filling all life

With its warm glow

32

Loves bondage shows

In theatric fare

With artistic license

Upon its stages

Loves discipline

Easy to find

49

Crossing lines

Made bare

Loves sadistic touch

Played in games

Theatrical farces

In content

Loves role playing

Institutionalized

Rigid stereotypes

Fixed reference

Like moths to a flame

Love is sought

By all walks of life

For its warmth

Its fire can burn

Flown blind into

Its heat can warm

Flown in orbit about

Its light beckons

Draws to its fire

Invites to a seat

About its flame

Its warmth lures

Its promise invites

Fall in love

Grow to love life

34

The fallen in love

Gone down to their graves

Rise in remembrances

Of those enduring

Never forgotten

By the eternal flames

Warmed beside

In loves embrace

Love is a wind

Fanning eternal fires

To roaring flames

In a banked fire

Borne on the wind

The fallen rise

To loves family tree

And enter love life

Tempered by discretion

Feast on love

Share its gifts

Indulge in its passion

Find loves light

To guide your heart

To loves table

However secret

The master is ready

To welcome family

To the love life

Filling creation

Love is inviting

Just capture the spark

Ignite the fire

Bank the flame

36

Loves games are played

On a battlefield

Antagonists, protagonists

In dogfights

Love games

Make some merry

Drive some mad

With their acts

Fools can get hurt

Get turned back

From loves sport

With wounded hearts

The wise grow

In their knowledge

Of loves arts

And license

Lick your wounds

Callous heart

Sadistic lover

Encountered

Tend the sparks

Kindled in heart

Bank the fire

Keep the flame

Don't lose the warmth

Learn the lessons

Love a gaming spirit

Be a good sport

Loves crowns reserved

To those enduring

Its celestial games

Its role playing

38

Let love guide you

To ancestral city

Containing nations

In universal laws union

An ancient citadel

Founded in the beginning

State of the art knowledge

Incorporated in its building

If at long distance

From city's sight

Warm by the fire

Of loves light

Reach it at last

In time you will

Arriving at length

To the end of your journey

39

In winter time

Love is reserved

To private parties

Out of public sight

A cold chill

Greets the heart

In winter scenes

To loves light

Greet the sparks

Fan the fire

To warm yourself

By loves flames

The fire lit

Winter endures

Warming heart

Tending the fire

40

Love nurtures

Stirs new life

In receptive hearts

To its light

Seeds grow

Flowers bloom

Fruits ripen

In loves warmth

Love invites

Be full of me

Make merry your heart

Your burdens will be light

Greet love

Where you find it

Your heart will be filled

Of its fire

Love in a nutshell

Crazed to madness

To fevered denials

Love may play

Fugitive from the heat

Of love life

Love may be

Running from the light

An able escape artist

It may slip from view

Taking on a secret love

Hidden from you

Be the nut cracker

Break through the shell

See the love hidden

From sight so well

42

Love is the balm

For world weary

Colored with love

Worlds transform

Antagonists play

At love games

64

Roles are played

On loves stage

Love the light

Guiding your sight

A den of love

Worlds become

Guide your view

With a secret love

Warm your heart

By loves fire

Theater writ large

Life becomes

Living in God

However glum

A poison pen

May've writ the score

One is enduring

In God secured

A comforter

And helper

In any scene

God can be

Turn to God

When artistic license

Laden's you

With its burdens

44

Author, author

The proper cry

In dire straits

Or evil eye

Behind the scenes

Beyond appearances

It's theater in nature

From comic to tragic

Team spirited

Two line ups

Antagonists, protagonists

Take the field

Scripted goals

Interactive play

Teamwork

In every scene

45

Experience produced

Deliberate and controlled

A mind plane creation

Like dreams in sleep

Experience a slave

Of mind's masters

Doing their bidding

Beyond appearances

Experience deceptive

Conceals control

Behind the scenes

In performance

Experience reflective

Of assorted perceptions

How accurate yours

On what dependent

46

All seeing

All knowing

All powerful

Mind masters

Behind every thought

Behind every move

Behind every scene

Beyond appearances

Consciously

Or subliminally

Involved in it all

Active participant

Unseen

With finite review

Unknown

In character acts

Divine being

Rogue can play

Chief adversary

Deity can be

Known

By its works

Revealed

By its acts

Delusional

Domineering

Dualism

Creation can be

Separation

Segregation

From creation

Deity may foster

48

Star crossed lovers

Master and pupil

Family and members

In creation may be

Forbidden love

Denied knowledge

Separate lives

Given to live

Social relations

With hierarchy

External authorities

Given for life

Mortal

Vulnerable

Dependant

On environment made

49

From womb

To grave

Lifetimes lived

On the shady slope

Only hints of light

Reports of sunny slope

Reach the shade

In moonless skies

Lives in the dark

Lived in the shade

Nothing seen

As is in the light

Shadows in the cave

All that is seen

Never revealing

The source of light

50

Strength dependent

On developing gifts

Of psychic mind

For perfect measure

Bodily force

Guided by mind

76

Quantum measures enhanced

Reaches full potency

Otherwise adrift

In a sea of forces

Of varying potencies

Inferior and superior

Pecking order

Placement

Results of

Varying forces

Resident of mind

Reviewing mental life

Theater of the mind

Tempered opinions

Seeker quests

For confirmation

Of its view

Even afterlife

Journey begun

Death does not end

But new horizon

Places upon

Confessed communion

Fellow seekers can share

In their quest for light

For fatherland's heaven

52

All forces

Every power

Forged by mind

Beyond appearances

Nothing exists

But mind creations

Mind planes

All that's experienced

Life in mind

Mind powered

With mind machines

Reality's fabric

All else constructs

Of the mind

Behind the scenes

Of sophisticated action

53

Theatrical farce

Courtroom dramas

Police stories

States of law produce

Censoring acts

Painful penalties

Imposed deprivations

Punishments administered

No confession

Of higher court system

Of legal obligation

To grant harmless liberties

Theatrical fare

The life presented

Lived in the laws state

The staged jurisdiction

54

Ernest quest

Ernest aims

Fruits yield

Given time

Time to learn

Time to outgrow

82

Prior limitations

Of material dimension

Life in experiences

As experienced

Not probed beyond

Yields its fruits too

The beaten path

Conformity's road

Leads to the same place

Its followers

55

Threat of deadly force

And deprivations or pains

Binds the mortals

To laws conformity

The poison pen

Its prisons fill

With violators

Of prohibitions

Law written

Unbound to liberty

Its prohibitions multiply

By legislators opinions

Rights state grants

Not universal law dictated

Not across the board

In laws jurisdictions

56

The mind's entertainment

Theater fare produces

However altered

The everyday norms

Theatrical illusions

Mortality, pains and bonds

Are in mental life

Beyond appearances

Tricks of the trade

Theater farces

Bonds and blows

Performed on stages

The scene set quickly

The cast recognizes

Its performances role

And storyboard part

57

Antagonists feeding grounds

The stage can be

Players in a pool

To select from

Like a herd

Those on stage

May be preyed upon

By antagonists

States of law

Like great ranches

May have ranch hands

Offering protections

States of law

May shepherd

May fence in

For their care

58

The individual

Inverted pyramid

May be under

On life's stages

Daily routine

Hostile environment

Experiences demands

Spent meeting

Daily life

Preoccupied

External influences

Requiring attention

Famished spirits

Without spirit resources

Live lives

Of such distractions

Unsolved problems

Bad news

May star in the media

Of communication

Cooperation's lack

Key explanation

The worse plights

Resulting in

Money

May be the grease

On resources wheel

Required to eat even

Labor reduced

To pyramid scheme

Profit tiers

Of paychecks

60

Reading by candlelight

Scanning the heavens

For signs of light

For guidance

Searching texts

For records

Of prior seekers

Into mind

Looking for a path

To guide the quest

To mental life

To mind power

Fools or mad

To professionals

And even peers

Seekers are cast

The sun

Great engine of life

Invisible power

Feeds all life

How great a force

It bestows

Depends on intelligence

Applied in its light

A power source

Lighting the sky

Harnessed by mind

Yields great force

A power supply

Enduring its hospitality

It readily yields

Those applying

62

The light of the eye

In its color spectrum

How far from light

In the eyes of the beholder

Phases of the moon

Easier seen

Than lights range

Of experienced conditions

Water easier to know

Solid, liquid and gaseous

Than bodies of light

Possessing such conditions

Concentrated light

A cutting beam can make

What force light

Will you be

63

Underdeveloped

Limited potentials

Players granted

In theater fare

The quest

For natural force

For mind power

Overlooked

Daily life's demands

Daily routine

Has no time

Allotted it

Mythological

Superstitious

Madness

It is treated

64

Invisible powers

Like sunlight, oxygen

Support life

In a variety of forms

Invisible powers

Like language, knowledge

Empower living

To increased abilities

Invisible powers

Of space, mind

Enable living

To new potentials

Invisible powers

Extra influence

Applied to living

Provide an edge

Truth

As invisible guide

Leads to facts

From information

Truth

As invisible light

Guides the senses

To perception from sight

Truth

As invisible friend

Can be a comforter

In any scene

Truth

As invisible god

Can be an ally

In any situation

66

Invisible and beyond

Finite sense reception

Infinity is a living mind

And ancestral deity

The mind mature

Grown into life

Beyond appearances

Controls it all

Sweet dreams

And nightmares

The mind can produce

For its experience

Guided by intelligence

Life without end

In its potentials

Conformed to errorless acts

External infinity

Invisible mind provides

Subliminally connected

To all in review

Mind seated

Uniform potentials

Great equalizer

All life provides

Time travel

Teleportation

Levitation

Powers of the mind

Spontaneous healing

Materializing stuff

Psycho kinesis

Mind abilities too

68

Invisible friends

In your life

Should include god

Your ancestral deity

Invisible powers

In your life

Should include life's mind

Beyond appearances

Invisible assets

In your life

Should include your gift

Your connection to the mind

Invisible resources

In your life

Should include the infinite family

Its grand society network

Invisible lover

Mind becomes

To pupils of knowledge

Of life's great secrets

A secret love

Awaiting discovery

By reciprocal heart

Longing to meet

Lover's secrets

Looking to make

With heart yearning

For love's embrace

A life of love

Looking to share

With kindred hearts

Anywhere

70

Invisible starship

A communiqué away

The mind provides

Those of faith

Vast corridors

Full of provisions

Honeycombed

By population pockets

Connected by telepathy

And teleportation

City life makes

Of international unions

Infinite family made

And maintained

The starship waits

For faithful access

Invisible strength

Life's mind provides

By degree of faith

Possessed in use

Faithfulness full strength

Of mind provides

Lesser degrees lesser gifts

Of mind bestow

Knowledge a key

To mind's treasury

Experience a companion key

Confirming knowledge

Love a gift

Of faithful minds

In full strength

Experienced

72

Invisible companion

Seeing in life

Seeking acquaintance

Isolation with some take

Alone with the mind

The invisible accompanist

Seekers aspire

To a relationship

On a quest

To meet the mind

To make it a friend

Some devote their time

Greeting the mind

As all you experience

Another path provides

For a relationship

73

Invisibly

Powers that be

Exert influences

Over life's affairs

Silently

Without lifting a finger

Influences are wielded

In life's mind

A network of allies

In mind's family life

Can swing the scales

In your favor

Make the approach

Request an audience

With life's family

Is a beginning

74

Faithful membership

In universal court system

Liberty ensures

Throughout existence

Lesser faith

Appeals can make

For a hearing

With varying results

Degree of faith

Determining

Ability to receive

Courts response

Faithful

Fully able

To receive

Courts blessings

Experience's companion key

Required for knowledge's fruits

Beyond intelligence gains

Natural to learning

Experience confirms

That learned

When applied

In completion

Partial applications

Incomplete acts

Will not confirm or refute

Wisdom's knowledge

Invisible power

Transforming to deeds

Requires follow thru

In the act

76

Beyond appearances

Beyond experience

At times in your life

You'll find eternity

A hope and belief away

The other side of death

Eternity is waiting

Yours to discover

Like waking up

From a vivid dream

The afterlife is reached

From mortal lives

Death is only

A going to sleep

To wake up

In eternity

Think about this

Meditate on it

Life is like a dream

A plane in your mind

You can sleepwalk

Never aware of the mind

Beyond appearances

Behind the scenes

You can lucid dream

Aware of the construct

The realm of mind

You are living in

You can master mind

Develop your potentials

Transmit, receive, control signals

Composing the scene

78

Obstructive obstinacy

Self sabotage

Deliberate incompletion

Of nightmare potentials

Illusions like powerlessness

Or puppet theater

118

Or artificial environments

Of conspiracy potentials

The mind as adversary

Easily performs

Like a game

Of cat and mouse

The mind plane

Readily conforms

To dreamers control

Without adversary

In adversary's hands

In a mental illusion

Madness looms

Other side of lucidity

Lucidity reached

But unconfirmed

Madness invites

To the dreamer

Where psychosis lingers

Information illusions dwell

Easily slipped into madness

From lucidity you can go

Cling to lucidity

See the mind potential

Behind the scene

Beyond appearances

80

It's alive

Wherever you look

Whatever you see

It's alive

Connected to a mind

Sharing its potentials

Beyond appearances

Behind the scenes

All life an organism

Growing, reproducing

Creating, performing

Guided by intelligence

Every part with potentials

To be added to the pool

Joined to the body

Of active participants

New moons

Mind connections

Begin their course

In intelligence

Growing in light

Of psychic mind

To a full moon

Or eclipse

Starting a pupil

In an all seeing mind

Learning of reality

As external infinity

Streaming acts

Of the mind

All acts become

In infinite relativity

82

Blinding light

Experience can be

Information too

Can be blinding

Mere distances

The size of reality

Going on around

Can blind you

Infinity

A living mind

Everything guided

Can seem absurd

Easier the presented

The apparent view

Experiences explanation

Than infinite relativity

83

Between worlds

Between darkness and light

Between experience and mind

Historic miles can exist

Populations and professionals

Maps and mountains

Constitutional composition

Can lie between you and mind

A mountain of evidence

Supporting a library of volumes

Expressing the popular view

May exist imposing

Scaling a mountain

Of received information

May be required

To reach the mind

84

A natural gift

Mind bestows

A mental bandwidth

Sensory phenomena creation

Eyewitness to a dream

Possessor of thoughts

Knows mind powers

Knows mental abilities

Growing lucid in sleep

Realizing you're in a mind

Worlds and dimensions melt away

A new scheme warms the heart

Life becomes a star

Mind becomes God

Knowledge reaches singularity

Moonlight guides thru darkness

Ancestral deity

Personal godhood

Life's omnipresent players

A sacred trinity revealed

Life inside God

Life in a deity mind

Readily results in

Waiting to be discovered

Those ignorant

To mind behind life

Mind beyond appearances

May err religiously

Those probing

Beyond finite reception

Beyond measurable areas

Infinite mind can reach

86

Commitment

Relationship forming

For duration lengths

Regular engagements make

Marriage a peek

Consent reached by parties

Inclined to such affairs

As make hearts merry

Business an affair

Profits guided

A relationship

Commitment involving too

Socializing

Pleasant intercourse

Exchanging information

Commitment requires too

87

The golden rule

Governing life

In liberal measure

Behind the scenes

Its agents and courts

Possesses in good measure

Its states great unions

Of growing populations

Unheard of but not unheard

Discovered and order established

The golden rule enshrined

In temples, hearts and minds

Other legal bodies

Their courts and laws possess

Their agents and areas rule

Their portion of life granted

88

Degrees of faith

Different altars make

Before the deity of life

The ancestral mind

The high priests

Degrees of lucidity

Before the altar

May possess and serve

The worshippers

By degree of knowledge

Vary in their worship

Their praise reasons

The temples

In assorted design

Reflect the worship

Of their makers

Lovers conspire

In their hearts

To make life over

In loves images

Cupid's arrows poise

At every scene

Casting love's shadow

In every act

Filling life with love

More than meets the eyes

In the dark and cold

Of altered states

Love life

Easily joined

A gift of knowledge

Possessed correctly

90

Where the heart is

You'll find a maze

Built by mind

Traveled by thoughts

Life the expression

Of artistic deity

Its family power

An artists' community

Its liberal license

Friendly skies

To vision planes

About their business

A grid work

Streaming information

The composition

Of every scene

91

The games

Sliding scales

Degrees

Are formed for

Players in variety

Their acts present

To theaters stages

And media mediums

Dancers on the floor

The music hear

Steps well know

To the musical beats

The clowns and jokers

Greasepaint and costumes

Stereotypical know

And entertain with

92

Aspirant

In a garden's cave

Realizes the light

Hid behind every eye

The masters

At their games

139

In plain sight

Not confessed at play

Bubble inflated

The air treated

Infections guarded from

Sheltered living

Everything perfect

Product of intelligence

Works of an artist's craft

Beyond appearances

93

Characters perfect act

Yields to mugs review

A degree of light

Baring its muscles

Perfect performance

Artistic acts lead to

Mathematically perfect

Stereotypical art

Even the student

Degree of mastery attains

Pupil of artistic master

Its masterpiece due

Sleepwalking

Light is just there

Lucid, it reveals

In various brilliances

94

Degree of faith

In universal courts

In the golden rule

Determines results

Intelligence possessed

You know your rights

You can appeal

And measure effects

Experience possession

Grants resources

Buildings, authorities

The establishment

Hearing of them

You may wonder

Experiment with

Learn more about

95

Programs depending

On natural giftedness

Require use thereof

Even when unstated

Learning applications

Without methodology

You need be sensitive

To know how to do it

Going through motions

Without accompanying acts

Required for results

Can disillusion with

Most lessons ambiguous

In theaters realm

Education left off stage

Or above your head

96

Natural as movement

Much like waking up

Death leads to afterlife

In infinite reality affairs

Without hesitation

Or any exception

The expectation at death

Is that you ascend

The unexpected

Not unprepared for

Is to stand between lives

In death's doorway

A curtain call

A performance ending

A new beginning

Death's natural state

97

Time to spend

Planting trees

Forming memories

In fruitful pursuits

That between

Cradle and grave

Consciousness and ascension

Life and death

Enduring

Surviving

Or enjoying

Life presented

Information varies

Along with experiences

But infinite relativity

Is a uniform understanding

98

Shifting sands

Shadows course

Change can bring

To experience

Minor or major

Changes may come

Infinite relativity equips

For either occasion

Streaming sensory pixels

The common denominator

Of infinite relativity

To everything occurring

Sets of numerators

Reflecting achievements

In universal development

On intelligence charts used

99

Kept secret

Or suppressed

Or just over the heads

Infinite singularity's achieved

Knowledge universal

Transcending schools

And placements given

Constitutional characters

Those realized

The shared container

And endowments

Intelligence shows

Those avoiding

Or distracted

From the view

Show too

100

Knowledge love life

Leads to and produces

Mastery so warming

Of hearts and minds

Developments other

Produced too

For so inclined

As to abstain

A party system

General environment

Mastery leads

Whatever resulting

Escapes

Altered states

Indulged in

By the normal

101

The sun, moons and stars

Light the planes

Of mind domains

In infinite reality

Infinity the sun

Lighting external reality

Filling it with warmth

Nurturing all life

Moons casting

Their phases light

Lighting skies

And dark nights

Stars supporting

Life centers and cultures

Dot the heavens

Observed created

102

Every star

Like the sun

Warming, nurturing

Supporting life

Many traits of sun

Reflect in deeds

154

Without completely

Performing its part

Altered states

Have their lights

Support for a time

Provide their members

Life and variety

No strange bedfellows

Partners in time

On life's stages

Without external infinity

In plain sight

Or public knowledge

It is a discovery issue

Minus internal infinity

In everyday use

Applied to force

Web walking, feeding occur

Streaming sensory pixels

Not recognized and taught

Illusions can occur

Of constitutional matters

Without knowledge

Being shared and held sacred

Substitution of idols

And their words may occur

104

Worlds unknown

Floating in a mind

Moved by mind power

Illusions can make

Lacking confessions

Proving confirmed

Faithful marriage

Cannot occur

Knowledge is power

Of observation

Abilities to acts

Endowing of its pupils

Even a parked illusion

Knowledge reveals

To its students

Of sufficient degree

Mind power

Quantum particles

Relies upon

For ceiling capacities

Quantum fusion

Mind power

At ceiling capacity

Generates for use

Surface matters

Force capacities

Prior quantum fusion

Can be marvelous

Quantum fusion

Split second speeds

Maximum force field

And greatest power endows

106

Mind plane creations

Sensory phenomena projections

Virtual theater enclosures

Cast environments in their light

What not by extension

Creation of the presented

160

Method of manufacturing

An immersed in environment

Where immune to wonder

Looking at the vault above

If it exists in sight only

As well as that all around

A scene full of sensations

In the eye of a beholder

An independent existence

Does not prove to be

107

Realizing the potential

Of enclosure as extension

Of the enclosed reception

What proven not projection

What not conformed

Ritual reproduction

Manuscript copying

In unstated nature

How dependant experience

On observers perception

For mirror reflection

Of scene being shared

Psychosis and hallucinations

Prove the dependence

On perception of observed

For reflections received

108

Now in mind stuff

I bid you well

On your way to affairs

You know too well

From elsewhere you came

To learn from me

Of things beyond sight

Existing mentally

A brief tour, a short visit

To the dimension of mind

My work provides

You can return any time

On these pages

My verse presents

Psychic reality

An introductory course